Ripley's— Believe It or Not!®

GREAT AND STRANGE
WORKS OF MAN

A Byron Preiss Book

TOR

A Tom Doherty Associates Book
New York

RL 4.8 IL 011-013

The Ripley's 100th Anniversary Series:

Weird Inventions and Discoveries
Odd Places
Strange Coincidences
Wild Animals
Reptiles, Lizards and Prehistoric Beasts
Great and Strange Works of Man

Ripley's Believe It or Not!
Great and Strange Works of Man

Copyright © 1992 by Ripley Entertainment Inc.
Trademarks owned by Ripley Entertainment Inc.
Cover design by Dean Motter
Interior design by William Mohalley
Edited by Howard Zimmerman and Elizabeth Henderson

A TOR Book
Published by Tom Doherty Associates, Inc.
49 West 24th Street
New York, New York 10010

ISBN: 0-812-51287-1

First Tor edition: August 1992

Printed in the United States of America

0 9 8 7 6 5 4 3 2 1

INTRODUCTION

Welcome to the special Centennial Edition of "Ripley's Believe It or Not!", the most famous and best known entertainment feature in the world. The centennial series is designed to help celebrate the forthcoming hundredth anniversary of Robert L. Ripley's birth in 1993.

Ripley was one of the most fabulous and interesting personalities of the 20th century. He spent his life traveling the globe in pursuit of the odd, bizarre, and incredible-but-true stories that have filled the "Believe It or Not!" pages for over 70 years. During this period, more than 80 million people in 125 countries have been entertained and amazed by Robert L. Ripley's creation. In addition, millions more have marveled at the incredible oddities on display at the Ripley's museums in America, England, Canada, Australia, and Japan.

Ripley's amazing worldwide industry is a true American success story, for it started humbly with one man and an idea.

In 1918, the twenty-five-year-old Ripley was a hard-working sports cartoonist for the New York Globe newspaper. It happened one day that he was stuck for a cartoon to draw. As his daily deadline approached, he was still staring at a blank sheet on his drawing board when inspiration struck. Ripley dug into his files where he kept notes on all sorts of unusual sports achievements. He quickly sketched nine of the more interesting and bizarre items onto his page, and a legend was born. That first page was titled "Champs and Chumps." Ripley's editor quickly came up with a snappier name, and "Believe It or Not!" became an overnight sensation.

In 1929, Ripley published his very first collection of "Believe It or Not!" in book form. It was an immediate success. A few years later his feature was appearing in over 200 newspapers in the United States and Canada alone. But Ripley was just getting started. With financial backing from his newspaper syndicate, Ripley traveled thousands of miles in the next few years. He visited 198 countries, bringing back oddities, antiques, and amazing stories from each place he stopped. The best of these eventually wound up in his famous syndicated feature. The amazing truth is that Ripley supplied at least one "Believe It or Not!" every day for thirty years!

In 1933, Ripley collected many of his fabulous treasures and put them on exhibition in Chicago. Within a year, his "Odditorium" had hosted almost two and a half million people. They lined up around the block to see the displays of shrunken heads, postage-stamp-size paintings, treasures from the Orient, incredibly intricate matchstick models, and wickedly gleaming instruments of medieval torture.

Soon after Ripley died in 1949, his unique collection of oddities was gathered and displayed in the first permanent "Believe It or Not!" museum in St. Augustine, Florida. And, fittingly, Ripley himself became one of its more amazing items. A full-size replica of the man stood at the door, greeting all visitors and giving them a foretaste of the astonishing objects they would see inside.

Although Robert L. Ripley passed away, his work lives on. The Ripley's organization has ceaselessly provided daily "Believe It or Not!" pages through the decades, always reaching a bit farther for those fantastic (but true) stories that stretch the imagination. And they are still actively seeking more. If you know of any amazing oddity, write it down and send it in to:

Ripley's Believe It or Not!

90 Eglinton Avenue East, Suite 510

Toronto, Canada

M4P 2Y3

There are now over 110,000 "Believe It or Not!" cartoons that have been printed in over 300 categories. These include everything from amazing animals to catastrophes to *Great and Strange Works of Man*, the volume you hold right now. So sit back, get comfortable, and prepare to be astonished, surprised, amazed and delighted. Believe it or not!

HOLLAND'S NEVER-ENDING BATTLE

ONE OF EUROPE'S MOST DENSELY POPULATED COUNTRIES,
HOLLAND IS ONE-HALF BELOW SEA LEVEL WITH 30% OF
ITS LAND RECLAIMED FROM THE SEA. AS PROTECTION
AGAINST RAGING FLOODS, HOLLAND HAS BUILT A STORM-
SURGE BARRIER CONSISTING OF 18,000-TON-CONCRETE
PILLARS LINKED BY 18 FT.-THICK-STEEL GATES WHICH CAN
BE RAISED OR LOWERED ACCORDING TO CONDITIONS

THE *FENCE* of the Hardscrabble Estate, in St. Louis, Mo.
ERECTED AS A MEMORIAL TO ALL SOLDIERS
SLAIN IN THE CIVIL WAR, CONSISTS OF
THE BARRELS OF 2,000 RIFLES

FRANCIS A. JOHNSON
of Darwin, Minn.,
CREATED A BALL OF TWINE
THAT IS 38 FEET, ONE INCH IN
CIRCUMFERENCE AND WEIGHS
21,140 POUNDS

JUDITH WESTON of Bolinas, Calif., KNITTED A SWEATER **12** FEET LONG, **9** FEET WIDE, AND WEIGHING **18** POUNDS -- *USING 72 SKEINS OF WOOL*

THE FIRST MAJOR SUSPENSION BRIDGE A 580-FOOT SPAN ACROSS MENAI STRAIT, WALES, *ITS DECK HUNG FROM 16 WROUGHT IRON CHAINS* ... IT SURVIVED FOR 115 YEARS

A **SINGLE FINGERNAIL**
OF THE STATUE OF LIBERTY
WEIGHS 100 POUNDS

MARK WOEHRER OF NEBRASKA INVENTED "TAG-A-LONG," A ROBOTIC SUITCASE CARRIER THAT FOLLOWS ITS OWNER WHEREVER HE GOES!

A MONUMENT
built in Moscow, in 1964, to commemorate Russia's achievements in space, is a 382-foot titanium obelisk *TOPPED WITH A ROCKET*

THE **CASTLE TOWER** of Oxford, England
WAS BUILT IN ACCORDANCE
WITH INSTRUCTIONS THAT
IT COULD NOT BE ROUND,
SQUARE, OVAL OR OBLONG

GEORGE WASHINGTON'S HEAD ON MT. RUSHMORE, S.D., IS TWICE AS HIGH AS THAT OF THE EGYPTIAN SPHINX

A HOUSE in Utrecht, Holland, OWNED BY HERMAN de WAAL HAS NO STRAIGHT WALLS

A **SKULL**
MADE OF CRYSTAL,
BY THE AZTECS,
BY LABORIOUSLY
RUBBING THE
SURFACE WITH
*STRIPS OF
DAMP LEATHER
DIPPED IN
SAND*

THE GREAT PYRAMID
NEAR CAIRO, EGYPT, HAS A BASE COVERING AN AREA SO LARGE THAT IT WOULD BE ABLE TO HOLD TEN FOOTBALL FIELDS... A SINGLE FOOTBALL FIELD IS 160 FEET WIDE AND 360 FEET LONG

A GINGERBREAD HOUSE
BUILT IN THE CLEVELAND (OHIO) CONVENTION CENTER, IN 1987, WAS 19 FT. HIGH, HAD THREE ROOMS, A FIREPLACE, A CHIMNEY AND 7,000 GINGERBREAD BRICKS. BUILDING IT REQUIRED 2,200 LBS. OF FLOUR, 2,700 LBS. OF POWDERED SUGAR, 3,000 EGG WHITES AND 1,965 LBS. OF OTHER INGREDIENTS

THE COLOSSUS OF CHIBA NEAR TOKYO, JAPAN, A 170-FOOT-HIGH STATUE OF THE GODDESS OF MERCY OVER-LOOKS TOKYO BAY

IN THE *FRANKLIN D. ROOSEVELT LIBRARY* THERE IS A PENCIL PORTRAIT OF ROOSEVELT *SURROUNDED BY AN EAGLE AND THE PLANET SATURN* MADE OUT OF THOUSANDS OF COLORED PENCIL SHAVINGS!

THE CASTLE OF FLECKENSTEIN, near Lembach, France,
--WALLS, TOWER, HALLS AND GALLERIES--
WAS CARVED OUT OF A STONE CLIFF 65 FEET HIGH

THE **FIRST** APARTMENT HOUSE
— CONSTRUCTED IN NEW YORK CITY —
ERECTED ON 18th STREET IN 1869
AT A COST OF $100,000,
WAS BUILT BY RUTHERFORD
STUYVESANT AND NICKNAMED
"STUYVESANT'S FOLLY" —
BECAUSE IT WAS FELT NO
ONE WOULD BE WILLING
TO SHARE A HOME
WITH STRANGERS

A **WATER WHEEL** ON THE ORONTES RIVER IN SYRIA IS STILL WORKING, ALTHOUGH IT WAS BUILT IN *THE YEAR 1000*

KRAK DES CHEVALIERS

THE GREAT CASTLE OF THE CRUSADERS NEAR THE MEDITERRANEAN PORT OF TRIPOLI THAT SALADIN, THE SULTAN OF EGYPT, COULD NOT CAPTURE IN THE 12TH CENTURY, IS SO WELL PRESERVED THAT EXPERTS BELIEVE **IT COULD STILL BE USED AS A STRONG FORTIFICATION**

THE **MAUSOLEUM**
NEAR LONDON, ENGLAND,
THAT HOLDS THE BODY OF
SIR RICHARD BURTON,
THE DISCOVERER OF
LAKE TANGANYIKA,
IS A MARBLE TENT

THE REVOLVING BALL IN THE MARION (Ohio) CEMETERY SLOWLY AND SILENTY TURNS ON ITS PEDESTAL

IN THE 1840s
JOHN BANVARD
OF NEW YORK CITY,
    PAINTED A SCENE
THAT SHOWED 1,200 MILES
    OF COUNTRYSIDE - THE ENTIRE
LENGTH OF THE MISSISSIPPI RIVER
- ON 3 MILES OF CANVAS!

A ROUND BLOCK OF MARBLE
IN THE PAVEMENT IN FRONT OF
THE TEMPLE OF HEAVEN, IN PEKING,
WAS REGARDED BY THE CHINESE
AS THE CENTER OF THE EARTH

CONICAL BASKETS MADE BY INDIANS IN CALIFORNIA'S SAN JOAQUIN VALLEY, WERE WOVEN SO TIGHTLY THEY WERE USED TO *TRANSPORT WATER*

EDWARD LEEDSKALNIN A LATVIAN IMMIGRANT WITH NO TRAINING IN ENGINEERING SINGLEHANDEDLY BUILT CORAL CASTLE, FLA., INCLUDING AN OBELISK WEIGHING 28½ TONS AND A 9-TON GATE THAT OPENS AT A TOUCH

**THE WORLD'S TALLEST
MAN-MADE MONUMENT**
THE GATEWAY ARCH in St. Louis, Mo.,
IS 630 FEET HIGH
AND CONTAINS MORE THAN 5,000
TONS OF STAINLESS STEEL

GAIL TURNER OF BELMONT, CA., BUILT A SMALL AIRPLANE FROM SCRATCH, FLEW IT FROM CALIFORNIA TO WISCONSIN, AND STORED THE PARTS IN HER LIVING ROOM--ASSEMBLING THEM IN A VACANT LOT WHEN SHE WAS READY TO FLY

MRS. MABEL C. WOOD
of Horseheads, N.Y.,
paints with oils on **COBWEBS**

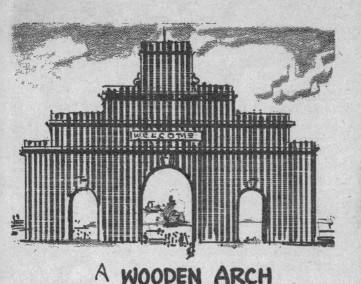

A **WOODEN ARCH**
CONSTRUCTED IN OTTAWA, ONT., IN 1860,
FOR A RECEPTION FOR THE PRINCE
OF WALES
CONSISTED OF
150,000
BOARD FEET
OF LUMBER
--*YET IT WAS
ERECTED
WITHOUT USE
OF A SINGLE
NAIL*

A FERRIS WHEEL CONSTRUCTED BY RICHARD GUETL, OF CHICAGO, ILL., FROM 14,000 TOOTHPICKS

THE ORNATE WAREHOUSE in Ypres, Belgium, WHERE THOUSANDS OF MILES OF CLOTH WERE STORED AND SOLD EACH YEAR, WAS 433 FT. LONG --THE BIGGEST CIVIC BUILDING ERECTED IN THE MIDDLE AGES

PAGODAS ON THE ISLAND
OF BALI
ARE BUILT WITH
ELEVEN ROOFS
--SO ELEVEN GODS
CAN BE OVERNIGHT
GUESTS IN
COMFORT AND
PRIVACY

THE BROOKLYN BRIDGE
THE NATION'S FIRST SUSPENSION BRIDGE BUILT WITH WIRE CABLES, CONTAINS IN THOSE CABLES MORE THAN 200 TONS OF DEFECTIVE STEEL --AND ITS NEW YORK TOWER RESTS ON SAND

THE EISENHOWER MEMORIAL TUNNEL
WEST OF DENVER, COLO., ABOUT 1.7 MILES LONG AND AT AN ALTITUDE OF 11,000 FEET ABOVE SEA LEVEL, IS THE WORLD'S HIGHEST ROAD TUNNEL

THE **WORLD'S** LARGEST CHURCH ORGAN
THE ORGAN
in the Church of Passau, Austria,
HAS 208 STOPS AND 16,105 PIPES

THE **CORNERSTONE**
OF THE WASHINGTON MONUMENT
WHICH WAS LAID ON JULY 4,
1848, AND WEIGHED 24,500 LBS.,
*DISAPPEARED AND HAS
NEVER BEEN FOUND*

MAHLON HAINES, A SHOE
RETAILER IN YORK, PA,
BUILT A FIVE-STORY GUEST
HOUSE *IN THE
SHAPE OF A
SHOE!*

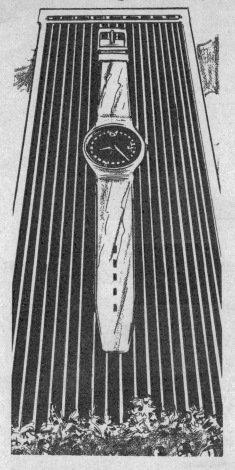

A HUGE WRISTWATCH HUNG FROM
A 37-STORY BUILDING IN TOKYO, JAPAN,
IS 37 FEET LONG AND WEIGHS
12,000 POUNDS

REG POLLARD OF MANCHESTER, ENGLAND, BUILT A 13-FT.- LONG REPLICA OF A 1907 "SILVER GHOST" ROLLS ROYCE USING 63 PINTS OF GLUE AND 1,016,711 *MATCHSTICKS.*

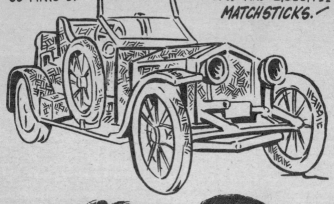

ANN HUNTER McCLOY   *and*   **EDWARD W. BALLARD**
BOTH OF VALENTINE, NEBRASKA, NEVER MARRIED ALTHOUGH THEY WERE FORMALLY ENGAGED *CONTINUOUSLY FOR 30 YEARS*

THE BUTTON KING
DALTON STEVENS OF BISHOPVILLE, S.C.,
HAS 300 BRIGHTLY-COLORED BUTTONS
ON HIS BANJO, 517 ON HIS SHOES,
3,005 ON HIS GUITAR, 16,333 ON HIS
CLOTHES AND OVER 100,000 ON HIS CAR

AN **ORNATE TOMB** in Jaipur, India, ERECTED BY THE MAHARAJAH *UPON THE DEATH OF HIS FAVORITE ELEPHANT*

THE WORLD'S LARGEST AIRCRAFT
THE C-5B OF THE U.S. ARMY AIR FORCE, IS 247.8 FT. LONG, HAS A
WINGSPAN OF 222.8 FT. AND *THE WRIGHT BROTHERS COULD HAVE MADE
THEIR ENTIRE MAIDEN FLIGHT INSIDE ITS 144.6 FT.-LONG CARGO
DECK – WITH ROOM TO SPARE!*

BIG BEN

LONDON'S FAMOUS CLOCK HAS 4 DIALS MEASURING **22½** FEET IN DIAMETER AND EACH CONTAINS **365** PANES OF GLASS..*ONE FOR EACH DAY OF THE YEAR*

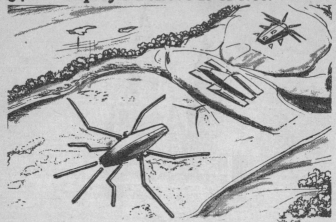

GIGANTIC WORKS OF ART

A CATFISH, FROG AND WATER STRIDER, RANGING FROM 18 FEET HIGH TO OVER 2,000 FEET LONG, WERE CARVED OUT OF THE EARTH BY ARTIST MICHAEL HEIZER ON A BLUFF OVERLOOKING THE ILLINOIS RIVER SOUTHWEST OF CHICAGO ···

THE HAMPTON COURT MAZE

NEAR LONDON, ENGLAND, THE WORLD'S MOST FAMOUS MAZE, IS ONE-HALF MILE LONG AND HAS BEEN CONFUSING PEOPLE FOR 300 YEARS, YET ITS SOLUTION IS SIMPLE — *SINCE IT IS ONE LONG CONTINUOUS HEDGE, KEEP EITHER HAND ON IT TO REACH THE CENTER*

A **CHURCH**
4½ FEET HIGH,
4½ FEET LONG
AND 3 FEET WIDE,
BUILT WITH
150,000 MATCHES
Created by
MIGUEL ANGEL
PRESSENDA
Parana, Argentina

IOLANI PALACE in Honolulu, Hawaii, BUILT IN 1879, IS AMERICA'S ONLY ROYAL PALACE

THE DESIGN OF THE NATIONAL CATHEDRAL IN BRASÍLIA, BRAZIL, WAS INSPIRED BY THE **CROWN OF THORNS** PLACED ATOP THE HEAD OF JESUS CHRIST

A **SILVER PITCHER** BY A PROVIDENCE, R.I., SILVERSMITH, WAS FASHIONED AS SMALL AS A FINGERNAIL FROM *A SINGLE DIME*

THE UNDERGROUND CHURCH
A CHURCH in Haute-Isle, France, 75 FEET LONG
AND 26 FEET HIGH, THAT WAS BUILT IN 1670
BY DIGGING INTO SOLID ROCK—
ONLY ITS BELFRY EXTENDS ABOVE THE GROUND

THE
**TRILITHON
OF ADYAR**
LOCATED IN
MADRAS, INDIA,
HAS TWO
ELABORATELY
CARVED DOUBLE
COLUMNS
--*EACH CARVED
2,000 YEARS AGO
FROM A SINGLE
BLOCK OF STONE*

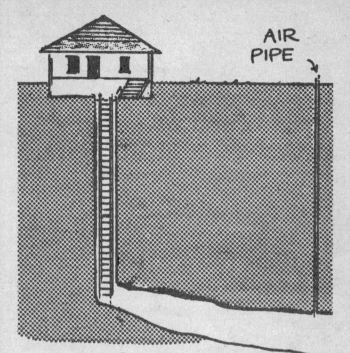

AIR
PIPE

NEWGATE PRISON
IN WHICH LOYALISTS WERE
CONFINED IN CONNECTICUT
DURING THE REVOLUTION,
WAS A FORMER COPPER
MINE *120 FEET BELOW
THE SURFACE*

BELIEVE IT OR NOT! *RICK HERNS* OF REDWOOD CITY, CALIF., CREATED A SCALE MODEL OF THE CITY OF SAN FRANCISCO—*OUT OF 54 LBS. OF PASTA!*

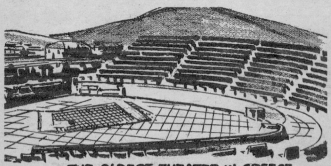

THE OLDEST THEATER IN GREECE
THE THEATRE OF DIONYSUS IN ATHENS, GREECE, DATES BACK TO THE 6th CENTURY B.C.

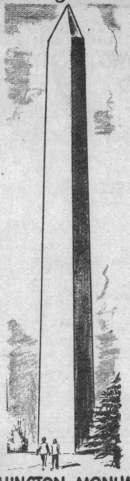

THE **WASHINGTON MONUMENT**
IS **555** FEET, **5** INCHES HIGH--
HAS A BASE **55** FEET SQUARE
--A PYRAMIDION AT ITS PEAK **55**
FEET HIGH AND WALLS THAT ARE
15 FEET THICK AT ITS BASE.

A VICTORIAN MANSION
EXHIBITED AT INTERNATIONAL PAPER
PLAZA IN N.Y.C. IN SEPT. 1985, WAS
MADE ENTIRELY OF ORDINARY
GROCERY PAPER SHOPPING BAGS!

SLEEPING BEAUTY'S CASTLE
BUILT BY 1,000 PEOPLE WHO WORKED ON IT FOR 5 DAYS IN AUG.
AND SEPT. 1985 AT PACIFIC BEACH, SAN DIEGO, CALIF., WAS 40.2
FT. HIGH AND CONSTRUCTED OF 15,000 TONS OF SAND

EUROPE'S FIRST SKYSCRAPER

THE WHITE HOUSE BUILT IN ROTTERDAM, NETHERLANDS, IN 1897, AN OFFICE BUILDING 151 FEET HIGH, WAS THE FIRST STRUCTURE IN EUROPE EQUIPPED WITH AN ELEVATOR. IT WAS SO STURDY THAT IT ESCAPED UNHARMED ALTHOUGH GERMAN BOMBS IN WORLD WAR II RAZED THE REST OF ROTTERDAM

THE U.S. PATENT OFFICE

FROM THE 1830s TO 1880, REQUIRED THE SUBMISSIONS OF DRAWINGS, WRITTEN DESCRIPTIONS AND TINY MODELS OF INVENTIONS THAT HAD TO FIT WITHIN A 12-INCH CUBE *NO MATTER WHAT SIZE THE ACTUAL CREATION*

MEZHIRICH, A TOWN IN THE SOVIET UKRAINE, WAS BUILT 15,000 YEARS AGO WITH HOUSES *MADE ENTIRELY OF MAMMOTH BONES!*

THE CANINE CASTLE

A TOWER 75 FEET HIGH
in the Castle of Chinon,
France,

WAS ESPECIALLY BUILT
BY KING PHILIP II AS A
KENNEL FOR HIS DOGS.

*3 TREES GROWING ON
THE TOWER WERE EACH
PLANTED AS A MEMORIAL
TO A DOG THAT DIED IN
THE ROYAL KENNEL*

A MAILBOX HOLDER

made by Eugene McLaughlin of Apache Junction, Ariz., in the shape of a roadrunner, is 23 ft. long with eyes made of two old hubcaps!

SACSAHUAMAN

A HUGE FORTRESS ABOVE CUZCO, PERU, WAS BUILT OF STONES AS HIGH AS **20** FEET--WITHOUT MORTAR OF ANY KIND--*YET EVEN TODAY A KNIFE BLADE CANNOT BE THRUST BETWEEN THEM*

A **HOUSE**
BUILT IN FRANKFURT-ON
-THE-MAIN, GERMANY,
*WITHOUT A GROUND
FLOOR--TO CARRY
OUT A STRANGE WHIM
OF ITS OWNER*

THE TRANS-IRANIAN RAILWAY
WHICH EXTENDS 895 MILES FROM THE CASPIAN
SEA TO THE PERSIAN GULF AND WAS BUILT IN
10 YEARS AT A COST OF $150,000,000
HAS 4,102 BRIDGES AND 224 TUNNELS, AND
*AT ONE POINT REQUIRES 6 BRIDGES AND
4 TUNNELS TO TRAVERSE ONLY 900 FEET*

THE MAUSOLEUM of MOULANA HUSAIN,
A MOSLEM SAINT, IN KERBELA, IRAQ,
WAS CONSTRUCTED OUT OF 15 POUNDS OF GOLD
AND 6,250 POUNDS OF SILVER   (1936)

RAY MURPHY
of Rapid City, So. Dak.,
CARVED THE ENTIRE
ALPHABET ON A LEAD
PENCIL IN JUST **40**
MINUTES-- *WITH A*
CHAIN SAW

THE CLIMATRON

A STRUCTURE AT ST. LOUIS, MO. BOTANICAL
GARDENS, HOUSES MORE THAN 11,000 PLANTS
IN FOUR DIFFERENT CLIMATES

ROGER PENFOLD BUILT A CIRCULAR
ISLAND HOME INCLUDING A
LIGHTHOUSE AND A TENNIS
COURT, OFF PORTSMOUTH, ENGLAND,
OUT OF A FORT THAT HELD
400 MEN.

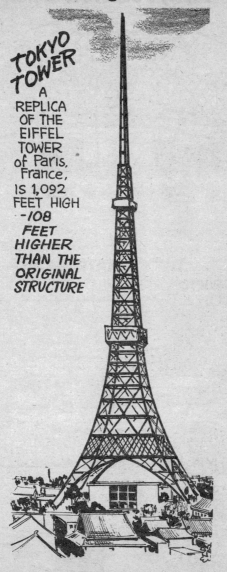

TOKYO TOWER A REPLICA OF THE EIFFEL TOWER of Paris, France, IS 1,092 FEET HIGH -108 FEET HIGHER THAN THE ORIGINAL STRUCTURE

THE HOUSE BUILT IN THE DARK!
FRANCIS A BURDETT - *TOTALLY BLIND* - BUILT THIS
THREE-STORY HOUSE <u>UNAIDED</u>
WAYNE, N.J
PRIZE WINNING SUGGESTION

THE **THOMAS EDISON MONUMENT**
IN THE IWASHIMIZU
SHRINE, IN KYOTO, JAPAN,
IS LOCATED IN THE
GROVE FROM WHICH
THE AMERICAN INVENTOR
OBTAINED THE BAMBOO
USED AS A FILAMENT
IN HIS FIRST
INCANDESCENT LAMP

The **CHAPEL OF REMONOT**
France
EXCEPT FOR ITS BELFRY
IS COMPLETELY UNDERGROUND
IT WAS CARVED OUT OF
SOLID ROCK IN ANCIENT
TIMES AS A PROTECTION
AGAINST PAGAN ATTACKS

THE **STRUCTURE** IN WHICH ARAKANESE
CHIEFS, IN EASTERN PAKISTAN, CELEBRATE
THEIR BIRTHDAYS IS AN ELABORATE BAMBOO
MAZE **330** FEET HIGH, THE LUMBER FOR
WHICH IS FLOATED DOWN THE SANGU RIVER
ON A RAFT 260 FEET LONG—
THE HUGE MAZE IS NEVER USED AGAIN

THE ROMAN COLOSSEUM
OPENED IN 80 A.D. TO GLADIATOR BATTLES AND OTHER
SPECTACLES, HAD NUMBERED SEATS FOR 50,000 AND
USED ADMISSION TICKETS MADE OF CLAY

THE OLDEST HOTEL
IN ALL GERMANY
THE GIANT, in Miltenberg,
OPENED FOR BUSINESS AS
A HOTEL IN **1590**

A SAND CASTLE

BUILT BY MICHAEL S. DI PERSIO OF BRADLEY BEACH, N.J., *WAS 8 FEET, 2 INCHES HIGH, COMPRISED 33 FLOORS AND HAD 1,637 WINDOWS, 84 DOORS AND 752 STEPS*

LUDWIG II

OF BAVARIA (1778-1848) *HAD AN ARTIFICIAL LAKE BUILT ON THE THIRD FLOOR OF HIS MUNICH APARTMENT, WHERE HE FLOATED IN A SWAN-SHAPED GONDOLA TO THE MUSIC OF A HIDDEN ORCHESTRA!*

A GIANT BUDDHA
AT YUNG HO KUNG LAMASERY
in Peiping, China,
60 FEET HIGH,
WAS CARVED FROM THE TRUNK
OF A SINGLE TREE

THE **PAPER HOUSE**
Pigeon Cove, Mass.
A 2-ROOM HOUSE WITH
WALLS AND FURNISHINGS MADE
ENTIRELY FROM NEWSPAPERS

THE SLOANE SQUARE
SUBWAY STATION
in London, England,
IS THE ONLY TUBE
STATION IN THE WORLD
*LOCATED BENEATH
A RIVER*

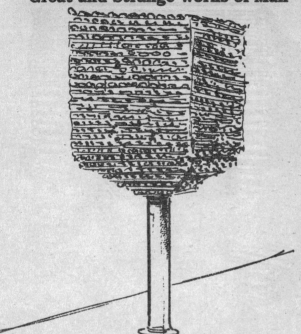

WALTER E. SCHNEIDER

of Monroe, Wis.,
balanced *5,555*
WOODEN MATCHES
on a one-inch-wide
test tube!

A BUILDING
IN ODEILLO, FRANCE
DESIGNED TO TAP SOLAR
ENERGY FOR HEAT AND
LIGHT, LOOKS AS IF IT IS
MELTING AWAY

THE ELEPHANTINE ROAD
ON THE ISLAND OF ELEPHANTINE, EGYPT, THE OLDEST HIGHWAY IN
THE WORLD, WAS CONSTRUCTED 4,700 YEARS AGO

THE **COLOSSI OF MEMNON**
at Thebes, Egypt,
HAVE ON THEIR PEDESTALS
THE NAMES OF GREEK TOURISTS
OF THE FIFTH CENTURY B.C.

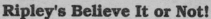

IN 1899 A PLUMBING SYSTEM INCLUDING A FLUSH TOILET WAS FOUND DURING AN EXCAVATION OF *THE ANCIENT PALACE OF KNOSSOS ON THE ISLAND OF CRETE!*

—A *GLOBE* CONSTRUCTED AT BABSON COLLEGE, IN WELLESLEY, MASS., WAS 28 FEET HIGH AND WEIGHED OVER 21 TONS

THE FIRST MILEAGE SIGN
A ROMAN PILLAR LISTING LOCALITIES AND DISTANCES ERECTED AT TONGRES, BELGIUM, 2,000 YEARS AGO

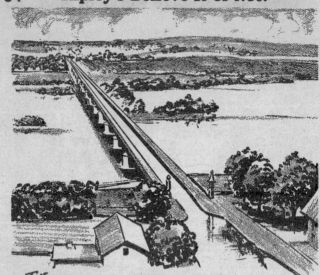

The **BRIARE SHIP CANAL**
Briare, France,
CROSSES THE LOIRE RIVER BY MEANS OF A BRIDGE 2,172 FT. LONG
BUILT BY GUSTAVE EIFFEL OF THE EIFFEL TOWER FAME

A FISHING VILLAGE EXCAVATED ON THE SHORES OF FEDER LAKE, IN WÜRTTEMBERG, GERMANY, CONTAINING 14 PREHISTORIC HUTS BUILT WITH BRUSH WOOD *STILL PERFECTLY PRESERVED AFTER 7,000 YEARS*

THE **GHORFA TENEMENTS** OF MATAMEUR, TUNISIA, WHICH REACH A HEIGHT OF 6 STORIES, LOOK *LIKE HONEYCOMBS*

2,200 WINDMILLS

IN ALTAMONT PASS NEAR SAN FRAN-
CISCO, CALIF., ARE PRODUCING OVER
20,000,000 KILOWATT HOURS OF
ELECTRICITY A YEAR.

THE **GREAT BUDDHA**
OF TODAIJI TEMPLE,
IN NARA, JAPAN,
BUILT IN THE 8th
CENTURY, CONTAINS
438 TONS OF
COPPER, 2 TONS
OF MERCURY
AND 880
POUNDS
OF GOLD—
*THE GOLD
ALONE HAS
A VALUE
TODAY OF
$2,032,800*

THE **OLDEST
SCULPTURE**
A MAN'S HEAD -
A TINY STONE
CARVING DIS-
COVERED IN
AFGHANISTAN,
*DATES BACK TO
ABOUT
20,000 B·C·*

'Now I think that you should know this charm-

IN 1937, ERNEST V. WRIGHT OF CALIFORNIA WROTE AND PUBLISHED A **50,110-WORD** NOVEL CALLED "GADSBY - A CHAMPION OF YOUTH" WITHOUT USING *THE* **LETTER E!**

A **GIGANTIC HEART**
BIG ENOUGH FOR A HUMAN 1,400 FT. TALL, MADE OF FABRIC, SERVED AS THE OCHSNER PAVILION AT THE 1984 NEW ORLEANS, LA., WORLD'S FAIR. IT IS 40 FT. HIGH, WEIGHS 2,000 LBS. AND, IN TIME TO A COMPUTER-SYNCHRONIZED HEARTBEAT, THE CHAMBERS, LIGHTED FROM WITHIN, SHOWING THE FLOW OF BLOOD PUMPING THROUGH THE HEART..

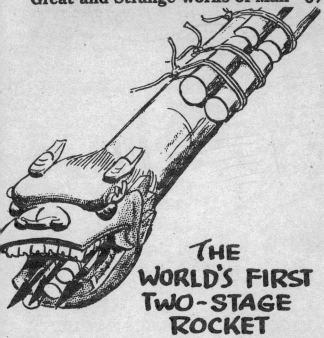

THE WORLD'S FIRST TWO-STAGE ROCKET

A "FIRE DRAGON" USED BY THE CHINESE IN 11TH CENTURY WARFARE, HAD A RANGE OF 300 YARDS AND ENOUGH DESTRUCTIVE POWER TO SET ENEMY SHIPS AFIRE -- THE ROCKETS, ON THE WAY TO THEIR TARGET, IGNITED FIRE ARROWS THAT FLEW FROM THE DRAGON'S MOUTH.

A VACATION DOWN BELOW

JULES' UNDERSEA LODGE (named after "Twenty Thousand Leagues Under the Sea" author Jules Verne) IS LOCATED IN A FORMER MARINE RE-SEARCH CENTER OFF FLORIDA'S KEY LARGO FOR $295 A NIGHT, GUESTS CAN ENJOY ALL THE COMFORTS OF HOME -- **WHILE GAZING AT LIFE UNDERSEAS, 30 FEET DOWN**

THE **RECLINING BUDDHA** IN THE WAT PO TEMPLE OF BANGKOK, THAILAND, IS 160 FEET LONG AND THE SOLES OF ITS FEET ARE COVERED WITH COMPLEX DESIGNS IN *MOTHER-OF-PEARL*

THE LEANING TOWER OF "PENCIL"

A GIANT PENCIL ERECTED IN TOULOUSE, FRANCE, TO PUBLICIZE AN ART EXHIBIT, WAS 49 FEET HIGH AND WEIGHED 660 POUNDS

THE WORLD'S SMALLEST WORKSHOP
GEORGE PERRAULT OF LOS ALAMOS, N·M·
HAS A COMPLETE HOME WORKSHOP -- INCLUDING
WORKABLE POWER TOOLS -- *ALL MINIATURES*

THE
*WORLD'S
FIRST
SKYSCRAPER*

THE HOME
INSURANCE
BUILDING
IN CHICAGO,
ILLINOIS,
10 STORIES
HIGH,

CONSTRUCTED IN 1884,
WAS THE FIRST SKYSCRAPER AND THE FIRST
BUILDING WITH SKELETON CONSTRUCTION
-- *WITH THE FRAME SUPPORTING THE WALLS*

A MINIATURE CHANDELIER

CREATED BY DON AND FRAN MEEHAN OF EAST WINDSOR, N.J., IS 4½" LONG, 3½" WIDE AND HAS 3,300 TINY PIECES OF AUSTRIAN CRYSTAL WITH 23 ELECTRIC BULBS THAT LIGHT UP!

A MANNED ROBOT
DEVELOPED BY
THE U.S. ARMY IN 1962,
COULD "WALK" 35 M.P.H.

IN 1990, "ROBODOC," THE WORLD'S FIRST
ROBOTIC DEVICE TO PERFORM SURGERY,
ASSISTED VETERINARY SURGEONS DURING
7 OPERATIONS IN SACRAMENTO, CALIF.!

STONE HEADS
CARVED BY THE OLMEC INDIANS OF MEXICO
3,000 YEARS AGO, AND WEIGHING 20 TONS,
WERE MOVED MILES THROUGH THE JUNGLE--YET'
THE OLMECS HAD NO KNOWLEDGE OF THE WHEEL

NATIVE GRAVESTONES
IN NDUMBI, ANGOLA, PORTUGUESE AFRICA, ARE SLABS OF HARD EARTH
CUT FROM TERMITE NESTS

GRACIE MANSION
IN NEW YORK CITY.
ONCE USED AS A STORAGE FACILITY, A
PUBLIC RESTROOM AND AN ICE CREAM
STAND, IS NOW **THE ONLY OFFICIAL
MAYOR'S RESIDENCE IN THE U.S.**

THE STEEPLE

of Our Saviour Church
in Copenhagen,
Denmark, can
be climbed by
copper-clad steps
which encircle the
*OUTSIDE OF THE
STEEPLE TO A
HEIGHT OF
200 FEET*

A GIANT PRAIRIE CHICKEN

erected in 1976 on Route 1-94 in Rothsay, Minn., when that
community was proclaimed prairie chicken capital
of the state, is 12 feet high and *WEIGHS 9000 LBS.*

Leutze's
FAMOUS PAINTING

"WASHINGTON CROSSING THE DELAWARE"
WAS PAINTED IN GERMANY ON THE RHINE - AND A
GERMAN WASHWOMAN POSED FOR THE FIGURE OF WASHINGTON

THE BOAT IS TOO SMALL TO BE ROWED THRU SUCH ICE WHICH IS | TOO THICK AND TOO PLENTIFUL
FOR THE DELAWARE - A BOAT THIS SIZE WOULD NOT SUPPORT 12 PEOPLE - IT WOULD BE
IMPOSSIBLE | TO STAND UNDER THESE CONDITIONS.... BESIDES THE FLAG | DEPICTED WAS NOT
CREATED UNTIL ONE YEAR AFTER THE CROSSING

DRAWINGS

CUT INTO THE GROUND IN THE
NAZCA REGION, 280 MILES
FROM LIMA, PERU, BY ANCIENT
CRAFTSMEN CENTURIES AGO,
ARE SO VAST THEY CAN BE SEEN
IN THEIR ENTIRETY ONLY FROM A
PLANE AT LEAST 1,000 FT. UP

THE LARGEST COVERED STADIUM IN THE U.S.

THE SILVERDOME in Pontiac, MI., which seats 80,400 people, is topped by a giant fabric balloon roof that covers 462,000 square feet and *IS SUPPORTED BY COMPRESSED AIR*

THE ICE PALACE AT THE St. Paul, Minn., ICE CARNIVAL OF 1888, WHICH WAS 140 FEET HIGH, *WAS CONSTRUCTED ENTIRELY OF ICE*

A **13-STORY CHINESE PAGODA** WHICH HAS BECOME THE EMBLEM OF THE AMERICAN YENCHING UNIVERSITY, IN CHINA, ACTUALLY WAS BUILT IN 1926 *ONLY TO CONCEAL THE UNIVERSITY'S WATER TOWER*

THE HIGHEST SUSPENSION BRIDGE IN THE WORLD EXTENDING FROM CLIFF TO CLIFF OVER COLORADO'S ROYAL GORGE IS 1,053 FEET ABOVE THE ARKANSAS RIVER

THE HOME of H.D. THARP, BUILT IN 1858, IN WHAT IS NOW SEQUOIA NATIONAL PARK, IS PRINCIPALLY LOCATED INSIDE A HOLLOW LOG— THE INTERIOR IS 56 FEET LONG AND 8 FEET HIGH

THE ILLUSION OF DEATH
AN OPTICAL ILLUSION CREATED BY
THE ITALIAN ARTIST GALLIENI...
VIEWED FROM A DISTANCE IT
APPEARS TO BE A SKULL --
*BUT CLOSE UP IT SHOWS
TWO CHILDREN PLAYING
IN A WINDOW*

THE **HOTEL** OF MATMATA, TUNISIA,
IS CONSTRUCTED INSIDE A CAVE

THE ROMAN AMPHITHEATRE
IN CAGLIARI, ITALY,
WHICH HAD SEATS FOR 25,000
SPECTATORS, WAS CARVED
OUT OF SOLID ROCK

THE STRANGE STONE BEDS OF THE SUDAN

RESTING PLACES CARVED IN THE SOLID CLIFFS OF THE SAHARA DESERT WITH STONE BALUSTRADES **TO ACCOMMODATE TRAVELERS WHO WOULD OTHERWISE HAVE TO SPEND THE NIGHT ON THE HOT DESERT SAND**

A **LIGHTHOUSE** BUILT BY THE ROMANS AT BOULOGNE ON THE NORTH COAST OF FRANCE, SERVED AS A WARNING TO SHIPS AT SEA *FOR 1,400 YEARS*

THE MONUMENT
IN GRACELAND CEMETERY, CHICAGO, ILL., OVER THE GRAVE OF WILLIAM A. HULBERT, FIRST PRES. OF THE NATIONAL LEAGUE, *IS A STONE BASEBALL*

THE **GREAT CASTLE of HIROSAKI**
in Japan
HAS STOOD FOR MORE THAN 300 YEARS
- YET ITS FOUNDATION CONSISTS
ONLY OF A PILE OF LOOSE
STONES WITHOUT MORTAR

THE "GREEN LADY"

A ROBOT AT THE FRANKLIN INSTITUTE IN PHILADELPHIA, PA., THAT CAN WRITE 3 POEMS AND DRAW 4 PICTURES, *WAS MADE IN 1805*

A TINY CAMERA

MADE IN 14 HOURS BY MASTER MINIATURIST HARVEY LIBOWITZ OF BROOKLYN, N.Y., STANDS ONLY 5³/₄ INCHES HIGH ON A COLLAPSIBLE TRIPOD AND *CAN ACTUALLY TAKE PICTURES*

THE **CAVES OF AJANTA** in India,
COMPRISE 29 MONASTERIES AND
HALLS OF WORSHIP CARVED OUT
OF THE ROCKY CLIFF AS
EARLY AS THE 2d CENTURY B.C.

A **CHURCH** 21" HIGH, 24 ¾" LONG AND 15½" WIDE CONTAINING 12 PEWS, COLLECTION PLATES, AN ALTAR TABLE, A LECTERN AND OTHER FURNISHINGS --MADE *ENTIRELY FROM 16,979 LINCOLN PENNIES*

CHAIN 500 FEET LONG MADE BY ELLEN TEMPLE, JAN BERNSTEIN AND JUDY CACCAMO ALL OF Bayside, N.Y., BY INTERLOCKING *OVER 12,500 GUM WRAPPERS*

AN **ORGAN**
BUILT FOR THE
CHURCH OF
LAS PIÑAS, IN
MANILA, P.I.,
ENTIRELY OF
BAMBOO
1790

BIRBAL'S HOUSE
in Fatehpur, India, A PALACE CONSTRUCTED
FOR HIS DAUGHTER BY RAJAH BIRBAL,
*WAS BUILT WITHOUT THE USE OF WOOD
EITHER INSIDE OR OUTSIDE THE STRUCTURE*

THE WORLD'S STRANGEST NATIVITY SCENE
COMPLETE WITH REPLICAS OF THE HOLY CHILD, MARY,
JOSEPH AND STABLE ANIMALS, IS PRESENTED ANNUALLY
IN AMALFI, ITALY, AT THE BASE OF THE GROTTA SMERALDA
--THIRTY FEET BELOW THE SURFACE OF THE MEDITER-
RANEAN SEA, *WHERE IT CAN BE REACHED
ONLY BY DIVERS*

THE GASTHAUS
IN MITTENBURG, GERMANY
THE COUNTRY'S OLDEST HOTEL
IS ON THE SITE OF A ROMAN
INN BUILT 2,000 YEARS AGO

THE
**TRANSPORTATION
BUILDING** in Boston, Mass.,
USES NO FURNACE OR CONVENTIONAL FUEL IN THE
WINTER! THREE 250,000 GAL. WATER TANKS IN THE
BASEMENT ACT LIKE HUGE THERMOS BOTTLES
STORING AND DISPENSING COLLECTED WARMTH
THAT IS RADIATED BY OFFICE MACHINES AND LIGHTS—
—INCLUDING BODY HEAT FROM 2,000 OCCUPANTS!

A **STONE**
ISLAND IN THE TIBER RIVER, IN ROME, ITALY,
CARVED INTO THE SHAPE OF A SHIP WHICH
MADE A PILGRIMAGE TO GREECE IN 291 B.C.
*TO BRING BACK A SACRED SERPENT IT WAS BELIEVED
WOULD END AN EPIDEMIC SWEEPING ROME*
THE SERPENT ESCAPED AND SWAM TO THE ROCKY ISLAND
——WHICH THEN BECAME AN OFFICIAL SANCTUARY

SAMUEL PEPYS
(1633 - 1703)
WHOSE FAMED DIARY
ACQUAINTED HISTORIANS WITH
LONDON OF THE 1600s, WROTE
PORTIONS OF IT IN CODE AND IN
FOREIGN LANGUAGES, SO IT WAS
NOT COMPLETELY DECIPHERED
*UNTIL 200 YEARS
AFTER HIS DEATH*

AMERICA'S SWEETEST LADY

A CHOCOLATE STATUE OF LIBERTY, DONATED BY A SWISS CHOCOLATE FIRM TO THE STATUE OF LIBERTY FUND-RAISING CAMPAIGN, WAS 5 FEET HIGH AND WEIGHED 335 POUNDS

THE SEIKAN RAIL TUNNEL-
THE WORLD'S LONGEST RAILROAD TUNNEL
CONNECTING HOKKAIDO AND HONSHU, JAPAN, IS 33.46 MI. LONG AND DRILLED 328 FT. UNDER THE SEA BED AND 787 FT. BELOW SEA LEVEL. THE TUNNELING, WHICH COST OVER 30 LIVES, TOOK ALMOST 21 YEARS TO COMPLETE AT A COST OF $3,750,000,000

A **HOUSE OF CARDS**
CONSTRUCTED BY PAUL WARSHAUER
AND PAUL ADLER, STUDENTS AT THE
NORRIS UNIVERSITY CENTER AT
NORTHWESTERN UNIV., Evanston, Ill.,
*50 "STORIES" HIGH AND CON-
TAINING 7,725 PLAYING CARDS*

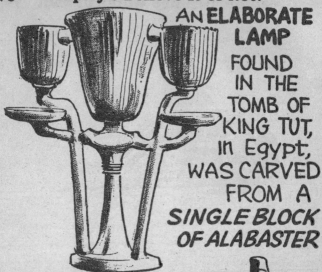

AN **ELABORATE LAMP**
FOUND IN THE TOMB OF KING TUT, IN Egypt, WAS CARVED FROM A *SINGLE BLOCK OF ALABASTER*

FISHHOOKS USED BY ALASKAN ESKIMOS WERE ONCE THOUGHT TO BE MORE EFFECTIVE WHEN CARVED IN THE SHAPE *OF A WIZARD'S HEAD*

SENA

A VILLAGE IN
Hadhramaut, Arabia,
CONSISTS OF A SINGLE
INHABITED ROCK

ROGER BOUCKAERT OF BELGIUM WORKED 5 HOURS A DAY FOR 4 YEARS TO CREATE A CROSSWORD PUZZLE THAT HAD OVER 50,000 WORDS AND WAS 30 METERS LONG!

THE **AQUEDUCT** at Segovia, Spain, BUILT WITHOUT MORTAR IN THE 1st CENTURY A·D·, STILL *SUPPLIED THAT CITY WITH WATER IN THE 20th CENTURY*

THE **CATHEDRAL** of **ETCHMIADZYN**
(Armenia)   ERECTED IN 303
BY KING TIRIDATES AND STILL
STANDING AFTER 1,667 YEARS
WAS THE FIRST STRUCTURE
TO BE TOPPED BY A CROSS

THE **GREAT GATE of SUNG CHUNG YO** China WAS CARVED ENTIRELY FROM A **SINGLE BLOCK OF MARBLE**—IT WAS COMPLETED IN 14 YEARS BY ONE MAN WORKING ALONE

THE **PYRAMID of CESTIUS** in Rome, Italy - 121 FEET HIGH, WAS BUILT AS THE TOMB OF CAIUS CESTIUS —WHO INSISTED THAT IT MUST BE CONSTRUCTED IN EXACTLY 330 DAYS

LOTTA'S FOUNTAIN in San Francisco, Ca., IS THE ONLY ONE IN THE U.S. THAT IS A MEMORIAL *TO A COMEDIENNE*

IT BEARS THE NAME OF LOTTA CRABTREE, THE RICHEST ACTRESS OF THE 1870s

AN ENDLESS
WOODEN
CHAIN
300 FEET LONG
WAS CARVED OUT
OF A SINGLE PIECE OF
WOOD
by *NICHOLAS BURTON*
- of New Bethlehem, Pa.

THIS CHAIN REQUIRED
MORE THAN 2 YEARS
TO MAKE

THE CITY WALL of Amelia, Italy, 2,800 FEET LONG,
HAS NO CEMENT OR OTHER BINDER
-YET IT HAS ENDURED FOR 3,400 YEARS

THE **HERMITAGE** of **ST. ADRIAN** WHICH HE CONSTRUCTED IN THE TUNNEL OF ST. ADRIAN, SPAIN, 1,400 YEARS AGO, NOW SERVES *AS A POLICE STATION*

THE ESCORIAL
A PALACE-MONASTERY NEAR MADRID, SPAIN,
*HAS 120 MILES OF CORRIDORS
AND 12,000 WINDOWS AND DOORS*

THE STAIRWAY TO SECLUSION
THE ENTRANCE TO THE CITY PARK,
IN COUTANCES, FRANCE,
CONSISTS OF 7 CUP-SHAPED LEVELS
SO CONSTRUCTED THAT A PERSON
ENTERING OR LEAVING WILL BE
HIDDEN FROM OTHER VISITORS

THE **GREAT** CANOPY OVER
St. PETER'S TOMB—in Rome—
IS SUPPORTED BY
4 BRONZE PILLARS
EACH OF WHICH WEIGHS
EXACTLY 27,948 POUNDS
BUILDER GIANLORENZO BERNINI
PLEDGED HIS PERSONAL
WEALTH AS A GUARANTEE
*THAT THE COLUMNS
WOULD NOT VARY
IN WEIGHT BY
EVEN AN OUNCE*

AT THE AMSTERDAM HILTON, GUESTS CAN RENT THE SUITE WHERE JOHN AND YOKO STAGED THEIR "BED-IN FOR PEACE" — THEIR FACES ARE ETCHED ON WINDOWS AND THEIR MUSIC *IS PAINTED ON THE CEILING!*

THE CN TOWER
in Toronto, Ontario,
rising to a height of over 1820 feet,
IS THE WORLD'S TALLEST SELF-SUPPORTING TOWER

MEMORIAL TO A MACHINE

THE FIRST STEAM ENGINE
in Bielefeld, Germany,
A 6 H.P. ENGINE USED BY A
DYER AND POWERED BY
HORSES FOR LACK OF COAL
WAS USED FOR 60 YEARS
AND THEN DEDICATED AS A
MONUMENT TO ITSELF

THE STREET OF THE LEANING HOUSES, Enkhuizen, Holland.
EVERY HOUSE ON THE STREET WAS BUILT 150 YEARS AGO—
LEANING TOWARD THE CENTER OF THE THOROUGHFARE

THE **NATIONAL MUSEUM** -Rome, Italy-
ONE OF THE WORLD'S RICHEST, WAS
ORIGINALLY BUILT IN 305 AS THE
BATHS OF EMPEROR DIOCLETIAN

RON KONZAK

OF BAINBRIDGE ISLAND,
SEATTLE, WASH., BUILT A
GIANT **23** FT.-HIGH
WOODEN HARP ATTACHED
TO A SOUND BOX SITTING
ON A **2**-TON CONCRETE
FOUNDATION ···*IT'S PLAYED
BY THE WIND ON 30
STAINLESS STEEL STRINGS*

THE CONCERT HALL ORGAN

in the Sydney, Australia, Opera House, designed by Ronald Sharp, has 10,500 pipes mechanically controlled through the action of a pedal board and five keyboards, but it can *ALSO BE OPERATED BY A MAGNETIC TAPE!*

A 300-LB. BATHTUB IN THE FUNABARA HOTEL ON JAPAN'S IZU PENINSULA, IS SHAPED LIKE A PHOENIX AND IS *SOLID GOLD*

THE STEEPEST STAIRWAY

THE **STAIRS** between High Town, and Lower Town, in Bar-le-Duc, France, RISE SO ABRUPTLY THAT THEY ZIGZAG FROM ONE STREET TO ANOTHER, SO THE CLIMBER WON'T SUFFER FROM VERTIGO

WINDOWS
IN THE HOMES
OF NATIVES OF
KAMCHATKA,
SIBERIA,
OFTEN ARE
CONSTRUCTED
BY SEWING
TOGETHER
*TRANSLUCENT FISH
SKINS*

DR. ROGER DOUDNA OF
FORRES, SCOTLAND, BUILT
AND *LIVES* IN A HOUSE MADE
FROM A *WHISKY VAT!*

THE **CUPOLA** of the Church of the Jesuits, in Vienna, Austria **IS NOT A CUPOLA AT ALL** IT IS AN OPTICAL ILLUSION, PAINTED ON A VERTICAL FLAT SURFACE BY ANDREA POZZO, IN 1703, TO ILLUSTRATE HIS THEORIES ON PERSPECTIVE

CHITRA
KALA RATNA GEORGE THARIAN
Emperor of Miniature Writers – Karachi, India
WROTE 26,779 WORDS ON A POST CARD!

THE GORGON SILVER COINS used in Macedonia 2,400 years ago, FEATURED THE DISTORTED FACE OF A DEMON *TO FRIGHTEN OFF ROBBERS*

BEEHIVES
USED IN HOFEL, SILESIA,
SINCE THE 1600s, *ARE IN
THE FORM OF PAINTED
WOODEN STATUES OF
MEN AND WOMEN*

THE
DEAN BRIDGE
A WOODEN
COVERED SPAN
in Brandon, Vt.,
WAS BUILT IN
1840 WITHOUT
USE OF A
SINGLE NAIL
--YET IT IS
STILL USABLE
131 YEARS
LATER

SYD DARNLEY of Sydney, Australia,
BUILT A SCALE MODEL OF THE SYDNEY TOWN HALL
USING 74,000 SEASHELLS

THE **RIDING SCHOOL
OF SALZBURG**
Austria
ORIGINALLY CONSTRUCTED
AS A BULLRING
CONTAINS 3 HUGE ROWS
OF 96 ARCADES EACH AND
*WAS CARVED OUT OF THE
SOLID ROCK OF A MOUNTAIN*

NEW GUINEA'S "BIG BIRD" MEMBERS OF THE DUK-DUK A SECRET SOCIETY IN NEW GUINEA DON COSTUMES AND PAINTED HEADDRESSES *TO FRIGHTEN WRONGDOERS*

A GIANT SAND SCULPTURE OF POPE JOHN PAUL II IN GUADALUPE, ARIZ., WAS 18 FT. HIGH, NEEDED 110 TONS OF SAND AND WAS CREATED BY JORGE SALDANA – USING ONLY A BUTTER KNIFE, WOOD FORMS AND WATER

SILVER CROWNS MADE FOR CAPPING TEETH BY INCA INDIANS BEAR AN AMAZING LIKENESS TO THOSE MADE 500 YEARS LATER BY DENTISTS

THE STATUE OF LIBERTY
BEARS A LOOK OF SADNESS
BECAUSE SCULPTOR BARTHOLDI
PATTERNED THE FACE AFTER
THAT OF HIS MOTHER'S LOOK
OF SORROW WHEN HE LEFT HIS
HOME IN COLMAR, FRANCE, DURING
THE FRANCO-PRUSSIAN WAR.

THE MOST WIDELY RE-PRODUCED WORK OF ART

is George Washington's portrait which has appeared on billions of stamps and paper money!

THE FIRST OPEN-TOED SHOES
JEWELED REPLICA
OF AN OPEN-TOED SHOE,
THE HEIGHT OF STYLE
IN THE YEAR 615.

THE VICTORIA GATE
IN DUNDEE, SCOTLAND,
WAS ERECTED IN 1844 TO SERVE
ONLY ONE DAY AS AN ARCH
FOR QUEEN VICTORIA'S VISIT
--*BUT HAS REMAINED AS A
MEMORIAL FOR 128 YEARS*

THE ART

OF PABLO PICASSO (1881-1973), THE SPANISH-BORN ARTIST WHO LIVED IN FRANCE MOST OF HIS LIFE, WAS SO HIGHLY PRIZED BY THE FRENCH GOVERNMENT THAT WHEN HE DIED IT AGREED TO ACCEPT MANY OF HIS PAINTINGS IN LIEU OF TAXES

QUADRICYCLE FIRE ENGINES
INTRODUCED IN PARIS, FRANCE, IN 1896 *PROVED FASTER THAN HORSE-DRAWN EQUIPMENT* THE FIREMEN, BY PEDALING WITH THE CYCLE ON ITS STAND, COULD THROW WATER **75** FEET

VISIT THESE RIPLEY'S MUSEUMS

Ripley's Believe It or Not! Museum
7850 Beach Blvd.
Buena Park, California 90620
(714) 522-7932

Ripley's Believe It or Not! Museum
175 Jefferson Street
San Francisco, California 94133
(415) 771-6188

Ripley Memorial Museum/Church of One Tree
492 Sonoma Avenue
Santa Rosa, California 95401
(707) 576-5233

Ripley's Believe It or Not! Museum
19 San Marco Avenue
St. Augustine, Florida 32084
(904) 824-1606

Ripley's Believe It or Not! Museum
202 East Fremont Street
Las Vegas, Nevada 89101
(702) 385-4011

Ripley's Believe It or Not! Museum
202 S.W. Bay Blvd.
Mariner Square
Newport, Oregon 97365
(503) 265-2206

Ripley's Believe It or Not! Museum
901 North Ocean Blvd.
Myrtle Beach, South Carolina 29578
(803) 448-2331

Ripley's Believe It or Not! Museum
800 Parkway
Gatlinburg, Tennesse 37738
(615) 436-5096

Ripley's Believe It or Not! Museum
301 Alamo Plaza (across from the Alamo)
San Antonio, Texas 78205
(512) 224-9299

Ripley's Believe It or Not! Museum
601 East Safari Parkway
Grand Prairie, Texas 75050
(214) 263-2391

Ripley's Believe It or Not! Museum
115 Broadway
Wisconsin Dells, Wisconsin 53965
(608) 254-2184

Ripley's Believe It or Not! Museum
P.O. Box B1
Raptis Plaza, Cavill Mall
Surfer's Paradise, Queensland
Australia 4217
(61) 7-592-0040

Ripley's Believe It or Not! Museum
Units 5 and 6
Ocean Boulevard, South Promenade
Blackpool, Lancashire
England

Ripley's Believe It or Not! Museum
Yong-In Farmland
310, Jeonda-Ri, Pogok-Myon
Yongin-Gun, Kyonggi-do, Korea

Ripley's Believe It or Not! Museum
Aunque Ud. No Lo Crea de Ripley
Londres No. 4
Col. Juarez
C.P. 06600 Mexico, D.F.

Ripley's Believe It or Not! Museum
4960 Clifton Hill
Niagara Falls, Ontario, L2G 3N4
(416) 356-2238

Ripley's Believe It or Not! Museum
Cranberry Village
Cavendish, P.E.I C0A 1N0
Canada
(902) 963-3444